WORKING WITH PARENTS
Building Relationships
for Student Success

Payne, Ruby K., Ph.D.
 Working with Parents—Building Relationships for Student
 Success. Excerpted from A Framework for Understanding
 Poverty Workbook. Second edition, 2005
 62 pp.
 ISBN-13: 978-1-92922-962-8
 ISBN-10: 1-92922-962-3

1. Education   2. Sociology   3. Title

Ruby K. Payne, Ph.D.

WORKING WITH PARENTS
Building Relationships
for Student Success

Table of Contents

Do not confuse having physical presence with parental involvement.

The research seems to indicate that when a parent provides **support, insistence, and expectations** to the child, the presence or absence of a parent in the physical school building is immaterial. Therefore, training for parents should concentrate on these issues.

WORKING WITH STUDENTS' PARENTS AND GUARDIANS

Think of parents not as a single group but as distinct sub-groups.

For example:

1) career-oriented/too busy to attend school activities.

2) very involved in school activities.

3) single parents working two jobs/too busy to attend.

4) immigrant parents with language issues.

5) parents with overwhelming personal issues, such as addiction, illness, incarceration, evading the law.

6) surrogate parents: foster parents, grandparents, et al.

7) children who, in effect, are their own parents; they no longer have involved parents or guardians.

In your campus plan, identify specific ways you will target each group. Many discipline problems come from students whose parents are in sub-groups 5 and 7. These students desperately need relationships with adults that are long-term and stable.

As a rule of thumb, the best (only?) way to make contact with groups 5 and 6 is through home visits, when and where possible. In sub-groups 5 and 7, the children/teens themselves are the *de facto* parents. Often they work full time in order to provide enough money for both the children *and* adults to survive. Time is a key issue for those students. *It is unrealistic to treat parents as one group. The needs and issues are very different.*

TIPS FOR WORKING WITH STUDENTS' PARENTS AND GUARDIANS

- Phone systems: Let parents and guardians talk to a real person. Phone systems at secondary schools often make it very difficult to talk to anyone.

- Have an awards assembly for parents.

- Identify a clear mechanism for getting information. For affluent parents, a Website is wonderful. For all parents, videos work. The videos need to be short and focused. For example, how to talk to your teenager, how to find out what is happening at the high school, how to get your child back to school after a suspension, etc.

- Another option is a predictable newsletter. But it needs to be simple, clear, and to the point—and it must include many icons or visuals so that it can be used whether you're literate or extremely busy. These newsletters can be posted outside the building in glass cases and updated weekly. They can be posted in supermarkets, Laundromats, etc. The National Honor Society could take it on as a service project. Newsletters can be mailed home, a better option than children carrying them home.

- Pay parents to come in and call other parents. Have a list of things to say and have two rules: You may not discuss teachers and you may not discuss students other than your own children.

- Have gatherings that involve *food.* For example, anyone can come to the school for 50-cent hot dogs.

- If you do parenting classes, don't call them that. Focus on the student: "How to help your child …" Many parents of teenagers are desperate for good information about teens. Teenagers are typically tight-lipped and, unless you have much opportunity to be around them, as a parent you may not even know what is "normal." Find ways for individuals with lots of exposure to teenagers to share that information with parents and guardians.

- Adopt a plot of land to keep landscaped and clean. One school in a very poor neighborhood did this. Parents took pride in it. (Some even planted tomatoes!)

- Divide parents up among all the staff members (secretaries included). Each staff member contacts those parents and tells them, "If you have a question you cannot get an answer to, you can always call me."

- Create emotional safety for parents by being respectful of their concerns, openly sharing school activities, clarifying behavioral parameters/expectations of the school, and identifying available opportunities.

- For all activities, organizations, handbooks, etc., use simpler formats for giving the information. Liberally use visuals to appeal to the illiterate, the immigrant, and the busy.

WORKING WITH PARENTS FROM POVERTY

The first issue to address when working with parents from poverty is mutual respect. The second is the use of casual register. The third is the way discipline is used in the household. The fourth is the way time is viewed. And the fifth is the role of school and education in their lives.

First, for many parents in generational poverty, school is not given a high priority. It is often feared and resented. Their own personal experience may not have been positive, and school is alternately viewed as a babysitter or a necessary evil (i.e., "If I don't send my child, I will have to go to court"). Second, when parents come in, because of their heavy reliance on a win/lose approach to conflict, they may begin with an in-your-face approach. Remember, they are doing this, consciously or unconsciously, as a show of strength. Just stay in the adult voice. Use language that is clear and straightforward. If you use "educationese," they're likely to think you're trying to cheat or trick them.

Use these kinds of phrases with parents from poverty (these are the types of comments they often use with their own children):

- "Learning this will help your child win more often."

- "The mind is a mental weapon that no one can take from you."

- "If you do this, your child will be smarter and won't get cheated or tricked."

- "Learning this will help your child make more money."

- "This information will help keep your child safer."

- "I know you love and care about your child very much or you wouldn't be here" (but don't say this if you don't mean it).

Discipline in generational poverty vacillates from being very permissive to very punitive. The emotional mood of the moment often determines what occurs. Also, in some cultures, the approach to boys is very different from the approach to girls. When the discipline is highly punitive, there is often a belief system that (a) the harsher the punishment, the greater the forgiveness, and (b) the harsher punishment will make the young person stronger and tougher. Consequently, the notion of a systematic approach to discipline usually doesn't exist. There is rarely mediation or intervention about a behavior. Generally, it is a slap and a "Quit that." If guidance is being provided to the parent about behavior, use a *WHAT*, *WHY*, *HOW* approach with visuals.

GETTING PARENTS FROM POVERTY TO COME TO THE SCHOOL SETTING

One of the big difficulties for many schools is simply getting the parents into the school setting. Howard Johnson, a researcher at Southern Florida University, has done work with why urban parents come to school. The first reason they usually come is a crisis. What he has found is that rarely do they come to the school for reasons that school people think are important. So the first question that must be asked when trying to get parents to school is: "What's in it for the parents?"

A study done by the U.S. government in 1993 with Chapter 1 schools looked only at schools that were 75% or more low-income. Administrators of the study then identified students within those schools who achieved and students who did not. They developed a questionnaire looking at criteria in and out of school to understand the variables that made a difference in achievement. Interestingly, whether parents actually went to school or attended meetings at school was not a significant factor.

What made the biggest difference was whether or not parents provided these three things for their children:

- *support*
- *insistence*
- *expectations*

SOME SUGGESTIONS (WHEN PARENTS FROM POVERTY COME TO THE SCHOOL)

1) Rather than the meeting format, **use the museum format**. That way parents can come and go when it's convenient for their schedule and their inclination. In other words, the school would be open from 6 to 9 p.m. Parents could come to one room to watch a video or a student performance. These would be repeated every 20 to 30 minutes. Another room could have a formal meeting at a given time. Another room could have board games for the students. Another room could have food.

2) **Have food.** Give gift certificates to grocery stores. These tend to be popular. Another favorite is clothesbaskets that have soap, shampoo, perfumes, etc., since food stamps don't always allow those purchases.

3) **Let the children come with the parents**—for several reasons. First, there often is jealousy or suspicion by the husband when his wife goes out alone. If the woman's children are with her, there is none. Second, school buildings tend to be big and confusing to parents. If the children go with them, the children help them find their way around. Third, a babysitter frequently isn't available. And fourth, children are natural icebreakers. Parents meet each other through their children.

4) ***Have classes that benefit parents***. For example: how to speak English; how to fill out a job application; how to get a Social Security card; how to make money mowing yards, doing child care, baking, and repairing small engines. Also, schools can make their computer labs available on Saturdays to teach things like CAD (computer-aided design) and word processing—simple introductory courses that last four to five Saturdays for a couple of hours.

ALTERNATIVE APPROACHES

 Use video. Virtually every home in poverty has a TV and a VCR or DVD player, even if it has very little else. Keep the videos under 15 minutes.

For all fliers home, use both verbal *and* visual information

 Provide simple, how-to activities that parents can do with children.

TIPS FOR WORKING WITH PARENTS FROM POVERTY

- Many adults from poverty didn't have a positive school experience. The greeting of the first staff member they encounter (secretary, aide, administrator, teacher) will either confirm their earlier experience or counter it. Some sort of building procedure and greeting should be agreed upon.

- Always call them by Mr. or Mrs. (unless told otherwise). It's a sign of respect.

- Identify your intent. Intent determines non-verbals. Parents from poverty decide if they like you based largely on your non-verbals. If they don't like you, they won't support you or work with you. For example, if your intent is to win, that will be reflected in your non-verbals. Likewise, if your intent is to understand, that will be reflected as well.

- Use humor (not sarcasm). They particularly look to see if you have a sense of humor about yourself. For example: Can you tell a story about yourself in which you weren't the hero? Can you poke fun at yourself?

- Deliver bad news through a story. If you state the bad news directly (e.g., your son was stealing), it will invite an automatic defense of the child. Instead, say, "Let me tell you a story. Maybe you can help me with the situation." Make sure you use the word *story.*

- If you're comfortable using casual register, use it. If not, don't use it. They'll probably think you're making fun of them.

- Be human and don't be afraid to indicate you don't have all the answers. As alluded to above, they distrust anyone who is "always the hero of his/her stories."

- Offer a cup of coffee. In poverty, coffee is frequently offered as a sign of welcome.

- Use the adult voice. Be understanding but firm. Be open to discussion, but don't change the consequences (unless new information surfaces or a better solution can be found).

- Be personally strong. You aren't respected in generational poverty unless you are personally strong. If you're threatened or have an in-your-face encounter, don't show fear. You don't need to be mean. Just don't show fear.

- If they're angry, they may appeal to physical power ("I'm going to beat you up!"). To calm them, say, "I know you love and care about your child very much or you wouldn't be here. What can we do that would show we also care?" Another phrase that often works is: "Are you mad at me, or are you just mad?"

- Use videos as a way to provide information and communicate with parents. Virtually every U.S. home in poverty has a TV, VCR, and DVD player. If possible, make the videos entertaining. They can be in any language, but they should be short.

- Story structure in generational poverty is episodic and random, and the discourse pattern is circular. Understand that these structures take much longer. Allow enough time during conferences for these structures to be used.

- *Home visits by teachers are the fastest and easiest way to build a huge parent support base quickly.* They also significantly reduce discipline issues. Use Title I money to pay teachers to make phone calls and do home visits before there is a problem. (The payoff from this one simple activity is tremendous.)

- Remember, the parents from poverty talked about you in the neighborhood before they came to see you. They often made outrageous comments about what they were going to say and do to you before they went to the school (entertainment is an important part of the culture of poverty). So when they return to the neighborhood, they have to report back. Some comments you may end up hearing will be so outrageous that they should be ignored. They were made because they told people in the neighborhood they were going to do so.

- As you discuss situations with parents, ask yourself what resources are available to these individuals. Some suggestions won't work because the resources simply aren't available.

- In middle class, when a topic is introduced that the individual doesn't want to discuss, he/she simply changes the subject. In generational poverty, the individual often tells the person what he/she wants to hear, particularly if that person is in a position of authority.

- Emphasize that there are two sets of rules: one set for school and work, another set for outside of school and work.

- Don't accept behaviors from adults that you don't accept from students.

TIPS FOR WORKING WITH PARENTS FROM WEALTH

- Don't use humor—at least initially—when discussing their child or situation. If you do, they'll think you don't care about them or their child.

- One of the hidden rules in affluence is: "It's not OK not to be perfect." So identifying your personal weaknesses will not appeal to them particularly. They want to know that you are very good at what you do. On the other hand, if you don't know something, don't try to bluff your way through. They will usually call your bluff.

- Another hidden rule in affluence is that you aren't respected unless you're able to discriminate by quality or artistic merit. Wealthy parents won't respect you unless you have expertise. If you aren't knowledgeable in a particular area, read the experts or get a school district expert to sit in with you for the meeting.

- Don't use circular discourse or casual register. They want to get straight to the point and discuss the issue through formal register. They won't respect you if you waste their time.

- Do use the adult voice with affluent parents. Understand that they are skilled negotiators. Clearly establish parameters when discussing issues with them. Affluent parents often believe that they and their children don't need to follow or adhere to the "rules" of the organization. Be firm about those boundaries.

- Emphasize issues of safety, legal parameters, and the need for the student to develop coping mechanisms for greater success later in life.

- Understand that a primary motivator for wealthy parents is the financial, social, and academic success of their child. They're very interested in what you'll be able to do to help their child be successful.

- When affluent parents come to school and are upset, they likely will appeal to positional power, financial power, or connections ("I know the school board president" … "I'll call my lawyer" …). They also will attack the issues. Be prepared to articulate the issues, and use experts by name in the discussion.

- Don't be intimidated by the affluent parent. Do understand, regardless of your position, who is standing behind you to support you. If you have little or no support above you, make sure you don't paint yourself into a corner. Affluent parents will rattle the organizational "cage" in order to get what they want.

- Understand the competitive nature of wealth (especially among those with "new money") and the need to excel. Their children are expected to be the best. There tends to be disrespect for those in the service sector, including public service. However, if their child is happy and doing well, most of them will be incredibly supportive.

WORKING WITH OVERPROTECTIVE PARENTS

What is driving the protectiveness?

a. Child is a possession—defend your own no matter what they do.
b. Child is proof of parenting success—it's not OK not to be perfect.
c. Fear of loss—death, affection, loyalty.
d. Loss of another child—want to protect this child.
e. Change personal experience—"My mother never loved me."
f. Beliefs about parenting—"I just want to love him or her."
g. Emotional need of parent—loneliness, co-dependence, addiction.

 # QUESTIONS TO ASK

a. What is the very worst thing that could happen if we … ?

b. What is the very best thing that could happen if we … ?

c. What coping strategies could your child learn so that he or she could be more successful?

d. I know you love and care about your child very much. What can we do so that you know we love and care about him or her too?

e. Is there any evidence the fear is a reality?

f. How will this request help your child be more successful?

g. At what age will you allow your child to be responsible for his or her own actions?

Interventions

a. Reframing.
b. Using a story.
c. Establishing the parameters of school success.
d. Using other parents to establish perspective.
e. Establishing the parameters of parental interventions at school.

Appeals

Among affluent parents, an appeal to one of the following is effective: safety, expertise, legalities, or coping strategies to be more successful.

Among parents from poverty, an appeal to caring, winning, being smarter, or not getting cheated is effective.

CONFERENCING WITH PARENTS

A PROCESS

1. Stop the blackmail (if that is a part of the conference).

2. Listen. If needed, ask the parent to repeat the conversation and say this, "I am going to put this in writing and I want you to read back over it to see if I have gotten the main concerns. I will share this with the teacher and begin to work on this issue."

3. Pivot the conversation. Find out what the parent wants.
    "Are you just mad or are you mad at me?"
    "If you were queen or king, what would be your ideal solution to this?"

4. Establish the parameters, i.e. what the limitations of the situation are. (In some cases, you must get back with the parents after you have had a chance to find out the legal ramifications.)

5. Discuss options within those parameters.

6. Identify solutions.

7. Identify a plan. If necessary, put the plan in writing.

CASE STUDIES

CASE STUDY: ANDREA

Andrea is a senior in high school. The counselor has come to you with a concern. It is the third six weeks of the first semester and Andrea is failing Algebra II honors. Andrea needs Algebra II to graduate. You call the parent in to look at the possibility of Andrea taking regular Algebra II so that she can get the credit and graduate. Algebra II is not offered as a part of summer school.

Andrea's mother comes in for the conference. She informs you in no uncertain terms that Andrea will not switch to an Algebra II regular class. Andrea is going to go to Texas A&M, all her friends are in that class, and she will not be switching. You explain to the mother that she will not have a diploma if she does not get a credit in Algebra II and that without a diploma she will not be admitted into A&M. The mother indicates that Andrea's grades are not the issue. Andrea's friends are the issue, and she is not going to approve the change.

- What is driving the parent behavior?

- What questions would you ask the parent?

- What intervention(s) would you make?

CASE STUDY: ANDY SLOCUM

Andy is in fourth grade. He is one of the youngest students in his class because he was barely 5 in first grade. You like Andy. Mrs. Slocum, his mother, is always at school. The family is very affluent, and Andy is her only child. The gossip network has it that Mrs. Slocum was married before and had two children and lost them in a custody battle.

Mrs. Slocum comes to you in March and tells you that she wants to retain Andy in the fourth grade. She knows he is gifted, but his grades aren't high enough to be in the program. He has been making A's and B's. She wants him to have all A's. From your observations, Andy is a bright child, he is somewhat immature (in comparison to his classmates), but he is very likable, has a winning personality, and is athletically gifted.

You tell Mrs. Slocum about the research regarding retention. The counselor has a conversation with Andy. You talk to the teacher about Mrs. Slocum's request, and the teacher is appalled. You tell Mrs. Slocum that you will not recommend retention. She tells you she will go to the superintendent if you don't recommend retention.

- What is driving the parent behavior?

- What questions would you ask the parent?

- What intervention(s) would you make?

CASE STUDY: CHARLES

You have a school that is 95% low-income, and at the fifth-grade level you have instituted a decision-making unit. Charles is in fifth grade, and his mother calls you one day and says the following:

"I heard that school was teaching decision making. My son ain't learnin' it. I want you to tell him that he has got to quit stealing so close to home. He needs to go three or four streets over. I don't know what that boy's problem is. That ain't no kind of decision making. If he can't make better decisions, I'm gonna tell the neighborhood about how your school ain't no good. And why they spendin' all that time on makin' decisions when he still don't know how to add?"

- What is driving the parent behavior?

- What questions would you ask the parent?

- What intervention(s) would you make?

CASE STUDY: MICHAEL

You are walking back to your office after visiting classrooms, and Mrs. Walker comes running in the front door. "What is wrong with Michael?" she asks. Michael is her son who's in third grade.

You say, "I haven't seen Michael this morning."

"Well, he just called and said that there is a problem. I need to talk to him."

Michael is called down to the office. During the conversation with his mother, it becomes apparent that Michael is angry with his teacher. He asked to get a drink of water, and instead went to the pay phone, called his mother, and told her to get up there right now. He's angry with his teacher because she gave an assignment he didn't want to do.

- What is driving the parent behavior?

- What questions would you ask the parent?

- What intervention(s) would you make?

CASE STUDY: MRS. SMITH

Mrs. Smith is a loud, gossiping parent who is active in the PTO. She has a son and a daughter. The son receives the focus of her attention. Yesterday Mrs. Smith called you because she is furious with you. She wants to know why you didn't do something about those students who put her fifth-grade son, Sam, in the trashcan at lunch. She tells you that if you don't do something about it, she will send her husband up there to "get you."

You aren't as concerned about that as you are that Mrs. Smith will go to the superintendent again with a badly skewed story.

You are surprised. The aides in the lunchroom are excellent, and you haven't heard anything about anyone being put in a trashcan. You talk to the fifth-grade teachers and the aides. No one heard anything about this, nor did they see anything.

So you call Sam in and talk to him. You ask for details about the incident—when, where, who. The details are very fuzzy: No, it wasn't during lunch, it was in the hall. He couldn't remember the names; they stuffed him in there before he could see them.

You probe some more. Finally, Sam says, "Every night when I go home my mom asks me what bad thing happened at school today. If I say nothing, she tells me I'm lying to her. So I decided to tell her I got put in a trashcan."

You recall incident after incident where Mom "rescues" Sam and threatens to send Dad up to see you if you don't do what she wants.

- What is driving the parent behavior?

- What questions would you ask the parent?

- What intervention(s) would you make?

CASE STUDY: MR. AND MRS. DESHOTELS

The second-grade teacher comes to you in January and tells you that Jacque has already had 25 absences this school year. The teacher has called Jacque's mother for an explanation, but the only explanation is that Jacque doesn't feel well. You look at her records for the year before; she had 36 absences in first grade.

You call the home and are unable to make contact. You get an answering machine. Finally, you send a letter, outlining the law about absences and stating your concern. You hear nothing. The next week, Jacque is absent another two days. You send a letter requesting a conference and indicate that if the absences continue without explanation, you will be required to take the next legal step.

You get a phone call from Mr. Deshotels. He cusses at you, tells you he will get a lawyer, etc. You find out from his monologue that he is a long-distance trucker, and you ask him if he knows how many absences his daughter has. He replies belligerently that he does. You say that you think 26 absences without a medical cause for one semester are excessive. Suddenly there is silence at the other end of the phone.

- What is driving the parent behavior?

- What questions would you ask the parent?

- What intervention(s) would you make?

CASE STUDY: MRS. BROWN

Mrs. Brown is a member of the Pentecostal Church, and she comes to see you about a novel that is being used in fourth grade. She is *very* upset that the school would have this book. The book is about a 12-year-old boy who goes on a hunt for a deer and comes to understand who he is. It's a book about coming of age and finding identity. She explains to you that the book is really not about a hunt, but the deer really represents a female and the book is about the sexual hunt. You tell her that the district has a choice option on books and that her daughter does not need to read the book; another book will be found for her daughter.

Mrs. Brown isn't satisfied and tells you that you don't understand. The book isn't suitable for any fourth-grader, says Mrs. Brown, and she will work long and hard to make sure it isn't read by anyone in fourth grade, adding that it's wrong to have a book like that in the schools. She has talked to her minister about it. Her minister is willing to go to a board meeting with her to protest the use of such inappropriate sexual reading in elementary school.

- What is driving the parent behavior?

- What questions would you ask the parent?

- What intervention(s) would you make?

Appendix

CONTRACT FOR CLASSROOM VOLUNTEERS

In order to protect my own child, I agree to the following guidelines:

1. I will not discuss any child other than my own outside of the school and/or the classroom. To do so is to violate the 1972 Federal Rights Privacy Act.

2. I will not criticize the teacher in front of the students.

3. I will not ask for confidential data about any student other than my own.

4. If I have a problem with something a teacher does, I can talk to the teacher privately. If I still am unsatisfied, I can talk to the principal about it.

I agree to these guidelines in order to protect my own child. If I do not follow these guidelines, I may be asked to not volunteer again.

_____
Signature

A NOTE RUBY PAYNE RECEIVED FROM AN ASSISTANT PRINCIPAL

I attended the Train the Trainers session in Houston in July. It was great. At the time, I had no idea how useful it was going to be when I was placed as assistant principal for the first time.

I am having a hard time in this school because there is a problem I've never had to deal with. It sounds like something Ruby could shed some light on, but I don't remember her covering it at the session. A large number of parents in this school *beat* their children when I send a note or call home about the students' behaviors. I have had to call [child protective services] many days after punishing a child. Staff members at school are as overwhelmed as I am. They say this hasn't been a large problem until just recently. Many are holding back on sending students to the office because of fear of how the parents will handle the child afterward. All of us are anxious for some guidance. Can you give us some information or recommend some sources where we can do some reading? We pray for both Ruby and divine guidance. You can e-mail me here at school or at home.

RUBY'S RESPONSE

It was great to hear from you and know that the training was helpful.

About beating children. Yes, this is a very common response in generational poverty, particularly in Caucasian and African-American settings. It is not as much of a pattern in Hispanic generational poverty, unless there are multiple relationships.

There are several reasons why parents beat their children.

First, many times the parents have only two voices—a parent voice and a child voice. To move a child to self-governance, a person needs to have a third voice, an adult voice, so that the child can examine choices. Many parents cannot do this because they don't have an adult voice. So they use the parent voice. And in conflict, the parent voice tends to be a very harsh, punitive voice.

The second reason they beat their children is that typically they don't know any other approach. Usually raised themselves under punitive parenting, they believe the maxim that to spare the rod is to spoil the child.

The third reason is that it's part of the penance-forgiveness ritual. If you believe that you are fated, then you really cannot change your behavior. So the greater the penance, the greater the forgiveness. You will often find that after parents beat their children (penance) they engage in a ritual of forgiveness. Forgiveness can include any or all of the following: cooking them their favorite meal; permissiveness; and giving them alcohol, cigarettes, part of the drug stash, and money. Or a parent might even come to school and chew someone out just to show their child that he/she is forgiven. The thinking tends to be the following:

- **I do the behavior because I am fated; I cannot change who I am.**

- **If I am fated, then I can't really change what I do.**

- **If I can't change what I do, then the real crime is getting caught.**

- **But if I get caught, then I am going to deny it.**

- **Because if I deny it, I might not get punished.**

- **However, if I do get punished, then I have also gotten forgiven.**

- **And I'm free to do the behavior again.**

I have some suggestions for you.

First of all, I would approach the situation differently. When an incident occurs, I would call the parent and say, "I need your help. We are asking that you use a WHAT, WHY, HOW approach to discipline, which will help us here at school. That is what we are doing. When your child does something you don't like, please tell him WHAT he did, WHY that was not OK, and HOW to do it right. *We want him to win every time and be smarter at school.* So to help us, please use the WHAT, WHY, HOW approach. (As a reference point for yourself and parents, make a little brochure or paper with this approach clearly shown.) Then say, "Please do not hit him. When you hit him, we are required by law to call [child protective services]. We don't want to have to do that. So please help us."

Parents do what they believe to be the right thing. Some will say to you, "Honey, you do what you have to at school, and we'll do what we have to at home."

Then you say, "I know you love and care about your child very much or you wouldn't be taking the time to talk to me. But I need your help, and I know you don't want me to call [child protective services]. So, for anything having to do with your child and school, please use the WHAT, WHY, HOW approach. It's a simple 1-2-3 deal. It's not easy being a parent, and we want you to be able to *win* as a parent. So please help us."

For the parents with whom this doesn't work, I would not call home or send notes anymore. I would look more for positive reinforcements than negative reinforcements. There is nothing we can do at school that is as negative as some of the stuff that happens outside of school.

Please stay in touch, and let me know how things are going.

TO DISCIPLINE YOUR CHILD/STUDENT, USE THESE STEPS

1) **STOP** the behavior that is inappropriate.

2) Tell the child **WHAT** he/she did that was wrong.

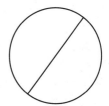

3) Tell the child **WHY** the behavior was wrong and its consequences.

4) Tell the child **HOW** to behave the next time.

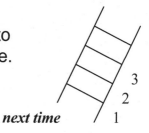

Ruby K. Payne, Ph.D.

No Child Left Behind (NCLB) Series ◆ Part IV

No Child Left Behind:
Parent and Community Involvement

By Ruby K. Payne, Ph.D.
Founder and President of **aha!** *Process, Inc.*
Part IV of a four-part series

An integral part of a principal's role is working with parents. Conflicts that arise because of time constraints, differing belief systems, and difficult social and behavioral issues consume a large chunk of a principal's time. Furthermore, in almost all legislation, parental involvement is now either required or considered to be a key component in improving student achievement. So how does a principal get parental involvement?

First of all, some concepts need to be revisited. There is no correlation between the *physical presence* of parents at school and student achievement. The correlation is between student achievement and *parental involvement.* So getting parents to physically come to the school is not a key issue in student achievement.

Second, another concept that needs to be revisited is the "one size fits all" approach, which only works when the student population is very homogenous. It doesn't work when the student population is racially or socioeconomically diverse.

The third concept is that our current scheduling of parental activities is fine—and that all activities must involve the parent coming in to the school. The scheduling and structuring of parental outreach and activities is often set up for the convenience of school personnel, rather than the parents, and is one-way, i.e., school personnel do not go to the parents. That needs to change.

The fourth concept is that parents actually have a support system that allows them to participate in school activities and that their experience with school has been positive. For many parents this is simply not true.

And last but not least, a concept among school personnel is that many parents are difficult. Tools to address difficult parents give teachers and administrators more efficacy and, therefore, often more success.

New Model to Involve Parents

This article is going to provide a model that involves the following: (1) niche marketing to parents; (2) building a layered, "community of support" approach (Wehlage, et al., 1989; El Puente Project, 2003) involving myriad interventions and different scheduling; and (3) tools for dealing with difficult parents, parents from different economic classes, and parent/teacher conferences.

PART I: NICHE MARKETING TO PARENTS

Niche marketing is a term used in advertising. Simply put, it means that one size does not fit all and that marketing needs to be targeted at specific audiences. The following table outlines some of the subgroups of parents found in many schools and ideas for involvement in their child's education. *A parent does not need to come to school to be involved.*

Put these activities into the site-based plan so that they occur. The activities actually become a marketing plan for the campus.

SUBGROUPS OF PARENTS	DEAS FOR INVOLVEMENT
Two-career parents	Put many things in print, e.g., fliers, newsletters, Web pages, etc. These parents will read and keep informed. Ask for e-mail addresses and send a monthly or weekly e-mail that updates them on the classroom and school activities.
Involved parents	These parents are at school, volunteering their help. The issue here is over involvement and parents wanting to take on administrative roles. Sometimes the boundaries involving student privacy need to be revisited.

(Chart continues on following page)

PART I: NICHE MARKETING TO PARENTS
(continued from previous page)

SUBGROUPS OF PARENTS	IDEAS FOR INVOLVEMENT
Non-working and uninvolved parents	This occurs at both ends of the economic spectrum. Phone banks where parents call parents and tell them about school activities begins a network. Home contacts are very powerful, as are coffee klatches (see Part II for explanation).
Surrogate parents	These are grandparents, foster parents, etc. They often need emotional support. Assign them a mentor—e.g., a counselor or involved parent—who touches base with them once a month.
Immigrant parents	Make short videos dubbed in their own language explaining how school works, how to talk to the teacher, what grades mean, what homework means, etc. Have the videos made by a person in your community from that immigrant group. DO NOT MAKE THEM TOO SLICK OR PROFESSIONAL because they will not be believed.
Parents working two jobs	Color-code the information you send home. White paper is "nice to know." Yellow paper indicates a concern. Red paper means that immediate attention is needed. You can call these parents at work as long as you do not talk at that time; ask them to call you back. Videos to introduce the teacher work well also.
Single parents	Structure activities that make life easier for the parent, activities that would include the children or child care, food (so they don't need to cook), or activities scheduled on the weekends or with open time frames rather than specific meeting times. Videos to introduce the teacher also work well here.

(Chart continues on following page)

PART I: NICHE MARKETING TO PARENTS
(continued from previous page)

SUBGROUPS OF PARENTS	IDEAS FOR INVOLVEMENT
Parents who are unavailable and students who, in effect, are their own parents	These are parents who are incarcerated, mentally ill, physically ill, traveling a great deal, have been sent back to their native country, have an addiction, etc. Teach the student how to be his/her own parent and provide linkages for the student to other school service agencies. Have the counselor have "what if" lunches where pizza is brought in and four or five students in this position discuss issues.
Parents who are "crazymakers"	There are only a few of these in a building (less than 1%), but they can destroy time and energy. These are the parents who constantly have a complaint. Each time a solution is reached, there is a new complaint. School personnel need to take their daily rate, divide it by 8 to calculate an hourly rate, and document the cost of personnel time used by one parent. No board of education wants to know that one parent took $60,000 to $70,000 of personnel time for no reason.

A part of site-based planning is to identify the percentages of parents who fit into these categories. If you have many parents in one subgroup, then it would be important to address more of those involvement issues.

PART II: BUILDING COMMUNITIES OF SUPPORT
The layering and structuring of "practices that contribute to student engagement and high school completion" is the basic concept in communities of support. "Chief among these is the ability of school personnel to create communities of support that are concerned about how students perform and express that concern in genuine, effective, caring ways" (El Puente Project, 2003). So how does one do that? One way is to create a scaffolding of interventions. The other is by creating linkages to community groups.

The following suggestions can help create communities of support for parents:

a) <u>Mutual respect:</u> Parents are welcomed by first-line staff. Parents are welcome in the building. Accusatory and blaming language is not present.

b) <u>School design teams:</u> A cross-section of staff, parents, law enforcement, ministers, and students who identify issues of support.

c) <u>Home contacts:</u> These are not home visits but quick five-minute visits to the home at the beginning of school to say hello. Substitutes are used to release teachers to do this.

d) <u>Videos:</u> These can be made by the staff and students to introduce faculty, to tell about school discipline programs, to highlight upcoming events, etc.

e) <u>Student and parent voices:</u> Through informal conversation (not meetings), parents and students are asked what the school could do to better serve them.

f) <u>Weekend activities:</u> Friday evenings, Saturday mornings, and Sunday afternoons work the best.

g) <u>Varied and targeted parental involvement activities:</u> Free donuts for dads the first Monday of every month. Carnations for moms. Lunch for grandparents. Picnics for people who live in the student's house.

h) <u>Support mechanisms for parents that involve follow-up:</u> 3x5 cards with the steps that will be followed. Magnets for the refrigerator that list school phone numbers and holidays. Stickers that parents can give to the child for good behaviors.

i) <u>Informal coffee klatches:</u> Counselor or principal asks a parent with whom they already have a relationship to invite three or four other friends over for coffee in the parent's home. The principal or counselor brings the donuts. This is a forum for an informal discussion about what bothers parents, what they would like to see, what they like, etc.

j) <u>Overcoming reluctance to participate by creating one-on-one relationships.</u>

k) <u>Tools for dealing with parent/teacher conferences.</u>

l) <u>Tools for dealing with difficult parents.</u>

m) <u>Simple written documents that have pictures and words and/or cartoons.</u>

n) <u>Using networking capabilities in the community:</u> Make a flier with cartoons that is one page and has an advertisement for a business in the community on the back. Introduce your faculty through cartoons. The advertiser pays for the paper and the printing. Distribute them to beauty salons, grocery stores, barbershops, churches, etc., much like a local community shopper or merchandiser.

o) <u>Information for parents that enhances their lives:</u> Offer information like how to fix bad credit (knowledge about money), how to manage a difficult boss (conflict-resolution skills), etc.

p) <u>Information on video or in cartoon that helps parents deal with their children, i.e., how to enhance obedience in your child.</u>

q) <u>Giving awards to parents:</u> A child identifies something a parent has done. On a Saturday morning the child gives a certificate to his/her parent and thanks the parent.

r) <u>Parent/teacher conferences led by the student.</u>

s) <u>Weekend activities that use the computers and athletic facilities of the campus.</u>

t) <u>Partner with a campus that has a surplus of parent involvement.</u>

u) <u>Peer-mediation training for students:</u> They teach it to parents informally.

v) <u>Teaching students to be better friends:</u> Have students list the five friends they go to when they have a problem. Tally who are the "best friends." Teach them how to ask questions to solve problems. Teach them how to identify which problems are serious and need to be referred, such as threats of suicide.

w) <u>Teaching parents to be better friends to other adults.</u>

x) <u>Block parties:</u> Get a street blocked off for an afternoon and have a party.

In other words, creating communities of support is a layered, varied set of interventions and activities. The idea that a school can have X number of meetings a year, a carnival, and a Halloween party is not enough. What must occur is a scaffolding of interventions.

PART III: TOOLS TO USE FOR PARENT/TEACHER CONFERENCES AND DEALING WITH DIFFICULT PARENTS

School personnel need to hone their conferencing skills to create a supportive environment for parents and develop conflict-resolution skills to deal more effectively with difficult parents. Our online questionnaires for new teachers have found that their two greatest issues are student discipline and dealing with parents.

Outlined below is a step sheet for the process to be used as a part of the parent/teacher conference, a parent/ teacher conferencing form (page 5), questions to ask to facilitate resolution of conflicts, and phrases to use by economic group.

Step Sheet for Parent/Teacher Conferences

1. Contact the parent. If it's going to be a difficult conference, have the principal or a counselor attend.

2. Make a list of items that need to be in the folder that is shared with parents: student work, grades, discipline referrals, rubrics, tests, etc.

3. If time is short, let the parent know about that and apologize for the time frame.

4. Have mutual respect for the parent. Ask the parent to tell you about his/her child. "As we begin this conversation, what would you like me to know about Johnny? You love him and care about him or you would not have come to see me." They know more

about the child than you do. Tap into that knowledge. Do not use "why" questions. Say "our child." (See below for questions to ask.)

5. Keep the conference focused on the data and the issues. "I have a folder of John's work. I would like to go through the folder with you and talk about his work." Or, if the student is there, "John is going to go through the folder and show you his work." Let the work speak for itself.

6. Ask the parent if he/she has questions.

7. Identify the follow-up strategies and tools to be used.

8. Thank the parent for coming.

Questions/Techniques to Facilitate the Conference

1. Stay away from "why" questions. Instead, begin with these words: *when, how, what, which.* For example: "When he did that, what did he want? How will that help him be more successful? How will that help him win? What have you noticed? How would you like to do the follow-up? Which way would work best for you? What is the worst-case scenario? What is the best-case scenario? How would you like to have this resolved? What plan could we use?"

2. STAY AWAY FROM STATEMENTS. <u>Use data and questions.</u>

3. Identify the fuzzy nouns and pronouns (*everyone, they, them, all the parents, all the students, women, men, kids, etc.*). If those words are in the conversation, ask this question: "Specifically who or which …?"

4. Identify vague qualifiers. Example: "It's better." ("Better than what?")

5. Identify fuzzy adverbs. Example: "He always has a bad teacher." ("Always? Has there ever been a time when the teacher was good?")

6. Identify the emotion in a statement. For example: "You're racist!" ("I sense that you feel the school is unfair and insensitive. Can you give me a specific example that would help me understand?")

7. Identify the hidden rules or beliefs (*should, must, can't, have to, ought to, should not, mandatory*). Example: "What would happen if you did? What stops you?"
8. Identify the parameters of the school. Example: "We do that to keep children safe." Or: "Just as we don't allow other parents to come in and tell us what to do with your child, we cannot allow you to dictate procedure for other people's children."

Phrases to Use with Parents

IN POVERTY	IN AFFLUENCE
This will help him/her win more often.	This coping strategy will help him/her be more successful in the corporate world.
This will keep him/her from being cheated.	Responsibility and decision making are learned behaviors. We can give him/her the competitive edge as an adult by learning these behaviors now.
This will help him/her be respected and in control.	This will keep him/her safe.
This will help him/her be tougher and stronger.	This will help him/her have the advantage.
His/her mind is a tool and a weapon that no one can take away.	This is a legal requirement.
This will help him/her be smarter.	This is an investment in your child's future success.
This will help keep you safe when you are old.	He/she will need processes/skills/content in the work world.
This is a legal requirement.	
I know that you love and care about your child very much or you would not have come to see me.	

CONCLUSION

The concepts that schools have used for so long to involve parents tend to be one-way, linear, and meeting-oriented. Just as advertisers have discovered that multiple messages and mediums are required to influence buyers, we must also use the scaffolding of relationships, interventions, activities, mutual respect, conflict resolution, and targeted assistance to create communities of support.

BIBLIOGRAPHY

Rosario, Jose R. (2003). *Final Narrative Report: September 1, 2002-August 31, 2003.* Hispanic Education Center, El Puente Project. Indianapolis, IN. Funded by Lumina Foundation for Education.

Wehlage, G.G., Rutter, R.A., Smith, G.A., Lesko, N., & Fernandez, R.R. (1989). *Reducing the Risk: Schools as Communities of Support.* Philadelphia, PA: Falmer Press.

Ruby K. Payne, Ph.D., founder and president of **aha!** Process, Inc. (1994), with more than 30 years experience as a professional educator, has been sharing her insights about the impact of poverty—and how to help educators and other professionals work effectively with individuals from poverty—in more than a thousand workshop settings through North America, Canada, and Australia.

Her seminal work, *A Framework for Understanding Poverty,* teaches the hidden rules of economic class and spreads the message that, despite the obstacles poverty can create in all types of interaction, there are specific strategies for overcoming them. Since publishing *Framework* in 1995, Dr. Payne also has written or co-authored nearly a dozen books surrounding these issues in such areas as education, social services, the workplace, faith communities, and leadership.

More information on her book, *A Framework for Understanding Poverty,* can be found on her website, www.ahaprocess.com.

Ruby K. Payne, Ph.D.   ◆   NCLB Series   ◆   Part IV

PARENT/TEACHER CONFERENCE FORM WITH STUDENT

Student name_____

Parent name_____

Date_____   Time_____   Teacher_____

PURPOSE OF THE CONFERENCE (CHECK AS MANY AS APPLY)
_____ scheduled teacher/parent conference
_____ student achievement issue
_____ parent-initiated
_____ discipline issue
_____ social/emotional issue

WHAT IS THE DESIRED GOAL OF THE CONFERENCE?

WHAT DATA WILL I OR THE STUDENT SHOW THE PARENT?
Student work, discipline referrals, student planning documents?

WHAT QUESTIONS NEED TO BE ASKED? WHAT ISSUES NEED TO BE DISCUSSED?

WHAT FOLLOW-UP TOOLS AND STRATEGIES WILL BE IDENTIFIED?

aha! Process, Inc.
P.O. Box 727
Highlands, TX 77562
(800) 424-9484
Fax: (281) 426-5600

www.ahaprocess.com

**Want Your Own Copies? Want To Give a Copy to a Friend?
Please Send:**

_____ COPY/COPIES of *Working with Parents: Building
Relationships for Student Success*

BOOKS: $5.00/each + $4.50 first book plus $2.00
for each additional book, shipping/handling

MAIL TO:

NAME _____

ORGANIZATION _____

ADDRESS _____

_____

PHONE(S) _____

E-MAIL ADDRESS(ES) _____

_____

METHOD OF PAYMENT:

PURCHASE ORDER # _____
Please submit signed copy of purchase order with completed order form.

CREDIT CARD TYPE _____ EXP _____

CREDIT CARD # _____

CHECK $ _____ CHECK # _____

SUBTOTAL $ _____

SHIPPING $ _____

SALES TAX $ _____
(only residents of Alabama, Florida, Georgia, Kentucky,
Nebraska, New Mexico, Tennessee, and Texas)

TOTAL $ _____

More eye-openers at ...
www.ahaprocess.com

- **If you are interested in more information regarding seminars or training, we invite to visit our website at www.ahaprocess.com**

- **Join our aha! Process News List!**
  Receive the latest income and poverty statistics *free* when you join! Then receive periodic news and updates, recent articles written by Dr. Payne, and more!

- **Register for Dr. Payne's U.S. National Tour**

- **Visit our online store**

    Books

    Videos

    Workshops

- **Additional programs/video series offered by aha! Process, Inc. include:**

    A Framework for Understanding Poverty

    Meeting Standards & Raising Test Scores—When You Don't Have Much Time or Money

    Tucker Signing Strategies for Reading

- **For a complete listing of products, please visit www.ahaprocess.com**